YOU'RE INVITED

to discover
    a predictable path to
        peace, joy, and freedom

WORKBOOK

Joseph Oquendo Saladino

You're Invited: to discover a predictable path to peace, joy, and freedom
WORKBOOK
By Joseph Oquendo Saladino
Copyright © 2019-2022 Healing For The Heart Ministries, All rights reserved.

Requests should be mailed to BRAM Publishing, 2998 E Springwood Dr., Meridian, Idaho USA 83642
Phone: 208-971-7570

Stories and interviews contained in this book are true, although names and identifiable information have been changed to maintain confidentiality. This book is designed to provide information and motivation to our readers. Its contents are the sole expression and opinion of its author.

The author and BRAM Publishing shall have neither liability nor responsibility to any person or entity with respect to loss, damage, or injury caused or alleged to be caused directly or indirectly by the information contained in this book. The information presented herein is in no way intended as a substitute for counseling or other professional guidance.

Paperback ISBN: 978-1-7341092-4-5

Subjects: BASIC: RELIGION / Christian Living / Spiritual Growth

Editor: BRAM Publishing
Cover Design: Fusion Creative Works & Rachel Langaker
Interior Layout Concept: Joseph Oquendo Saladino
Interior Layout Design: Rachel Langaker

For more information on how to purchase this book at quantity discounts, email info@h4hm.org

To connect with the author, email joe@h4hm.org

Published by BRAM Publishing
First Printing. Printed in The United States of America.

Table of Contents

Welcome — 5

Introduction — 7

Part 1: Laying the Groundwork — 11

RSVP — 13

Freedom Protocol — 17

Temptation and the Rules of Engagement — 23

Truth and Lies — 29

Contracts — 33

Ruling Over Sin — 37

What is Sin? — 41

Only by God's Authority — 45

Identifying the Lies — 51

Forgiveness — 55

Part 2: Practical Applications — 61

Let's Get Started — 63

Pride and Humility — 67

Hardship and Trials — 71

Vigilance and Perseverance — 75

Is Jesus Necessary? — 79

Lastly — 83

Acknowledgement — 85

Appendix: Forms — 87

Welcome

As the author of the "You're Invited" book, let me welcome you to a deeper understanding of the Freedom Protocol as you continue to discover a predictable path to peace, joy, and freedom. This workbook will help you dig deeper and transfer what you learned in the book to real life situations.

As you work your way through this workbook, you will find new tools that will help you rule over the power of sin without the white-knuckle experience we referred to in the book. You will soon be amazed at how you can predictably be free from overwhelming temptation and harassment by the enemy[1] of your soul.

I have been sharing these tools with my clients for years and it has been wonderful to watch them gain victory over the enemy and the power of sin in their lives. What you will be learning here is not theory or just theological concepts but rather practical ways to dramatically reduce the enemy's influence in your life.

By now, you should have the "You're Invited" book we will be using as the textbook with this workbook. At the beginning of the book, you will find two sections which you should read as an introduction. These sections are the Foreword and Full Disclosure. The remainder of the book, the fifteen chapters, in conjunction with this workbook will explain how the Freedom Protocol works and help you apply the principles in your own life. Each chapter is designed to provide you with practical ways to successfully implement the Freedom Protocol and to quickly get results.

Here are a few things you should remember as you work your way through the workbook:

1. This workbook will guide you on a journey which is designed to take time, so you can enjoy your relationship with God. This is not a trip where the sole objective is the destination. There is no rush. Take your time and experience all that God has in store for you. Don't settle for a mediocre experience with God.

2. The amount of effort you put into reading the book and working with the workbook will give you better results. As you move forward, keep in mind that when the truth sets you free, often truth can hurt a lot just before you get free. You are trying to get out of bondage to the enemy of your soul and he wants to keep you in bondage. Thankfully the Lord will fight on your behalf when you cooperate with Him.

---

1. Whenever the term "the enemy" is used in the book and in this workbook, it is Satan being referred to. The one who is the enemy of our souls and the one who seeks to destroy us whenever and wherever possible.

3. Always remember that you are not in this alone. That's good news and bad news. The God of heaven will be with you as you move forward with the book and workbook, and the enemy will also be right there attempting to undo your efforts in his desire to destroy your life and keep you in bondage. You have nothing to fear. The enemy of your soul will try many different tricks to keep you in bondage to his lies. As you move forward, you will discover and be exposed to these lies. Just stay the course, cling to the truth, and go where God leads you in this process. In the end, you won't be sorry.

4. Any effort you put into exercising the Freedom Protocol will not escape God's notice. You will be surprised how quickly God will answer your questions as you search for truth. He is with you in this journey and wants you to be successful. Don't settle for second best but go for all you can get throughout this journey.

5. Don't rush through this workbook. We certainly want you to complete each chapter, but we would rather you get a firm grasp of each chapter before moving forward. This is a bit like studying Algebra; if you miss the first few classes or don't understand the foundations at the beginning, then it will become more difficult later. Each chapter and section are designed to give you all the tools you need for the following chapters. It is better to fully understand one concept before moving on to the next one.

6. If you have any questions, feel free to contact us at info@h4hm.org.

7. Finally, be courageous as you move forward. Determine to stay the course and get the most you can from each chapter. As I tell my clients, I predict that your life is about to change in amazing ways.

You are now ready to start by reading the "Foreword," and "Full Disclosure" sections of the book. Before you start each Chapter in the workbook, be sure to read the relevant chapter in the book again as you progress through each chapter of the workbook. The forms you will need are in the back of the workbook. You can copy them with any copier. If you wish, you can download them from the H4HM website. Links to those locations are within the text of the workbook.

Get familiar with what the Freedom Protocol is and how it works. As you work your way through each chapter of the book and workbook, remember that you can always email us with your questions.

Let me commend you again for going deeper into the Freedom Protocol to get all you can from this process. Take your time and enjoy this incredible journey. You will be blessed as you strive to get the most out of the book and this workbook. Commit to exercising what you learn for at least the first 30 days. If you do, your life will never be the same.

Let your journey to freedom start right now.

Joseph Oquendo Saladino, Author

Introduction

1. Does the idea that no one can understand God help or hinder you in our walk with Him?
   _____
   _____
   _____
   _____

> *What if a change in our thinking, could give us more victory in our lives?*
> *What if we could be less harassed and tormented by the enemy, and/or not*
> *controlled by our addictions or the enemy's temptations?*

2. Do you feel that God is hiding Himself from you?
   _____
   _____

3. Do you feel that God is trying to trick you?
   _____
   _____

4. Do you struggle with understanding God?
   _____
   _____

5. What is difficult for you to understand about God?
   _____
   _____

6. Do you recognize times in your life when you struggled with lies about who God is? Can you identify two lies:

　_____
　_____
　_____
　_____

7. What does "white knuckling" your way through life look like to you?

　_____
　_____
　_____
　_____

8. On a scale of 0 to 10, how much of the abundant life would you say you're living right now?

　　　0 — 1 — 2 — 3 — 4 — 5 — 6 — 7 — 8 — 9 — 10

9. What should victory over sin look like in your walk with God?

　_____
　_____
　_____
　_____

10. On a scale of 0 to 10, how much are you "white knuckling" your way through life?

　　　0 — 1 — 2 — 3 — 4 — 5 — 6 — 7 — 8 — 9 — 10

11. On a scale of 0 to 10, how much are you being harassed by the enemy?

　　　0 — 1 — 2 — 3 — 4 — 5 — 6 — 7 — 8 — 9 — 10

12. Describe your desired relationship with God.

　_____
　_____
　_____
　_____

Notes:

For your thoughts, insights, and questions . . .

PART 1:

Laying the Groundwork

Chapter One:

RSVP

This chapter is an overview of the "You're Invited:" book. It will give you a general overview of what is ahead as we continue to go deeper into the Freedom Protocol. While this chapter is short, this chapter will hopefully help you identify the areas of your greatest need and expectations regarding the Freedom Protocol.

1. Have you ever experienced despair? If so, can you identify what led up to it?

   _____
   _____
   _____
   _____
   _____

2. Are there things in your life that have brought you to the point of despair for which you would like God's help? Pick the top three:

   _____
   _____
   _____
   _____
   _____

3. When you see the word "Victory" what are your first thoughts or feelings about that word?

   _____
   _____
   _____
   _____
   _____

4. Do you feel at times that the plan of salvation is complicated?

5. Do you feel life is complicated at times?

6. Do you feel like there is always more required to be saved?

7. Which items listed at the bottom of pg. 18 in the book strike a chord with you?

8. Are there some other life difficulties not listed on pg. 18 of the book with which you desire success in your life?

Keep this list in your mind as you move forward in the book and this workbook. If you need help addressing your specific unaddressed needs, please contact your instructor or the author. We are committed to your success, and we want you to personally discover and experience the abundant life.

Notes:

For your thoughts, insights, and questions . . .

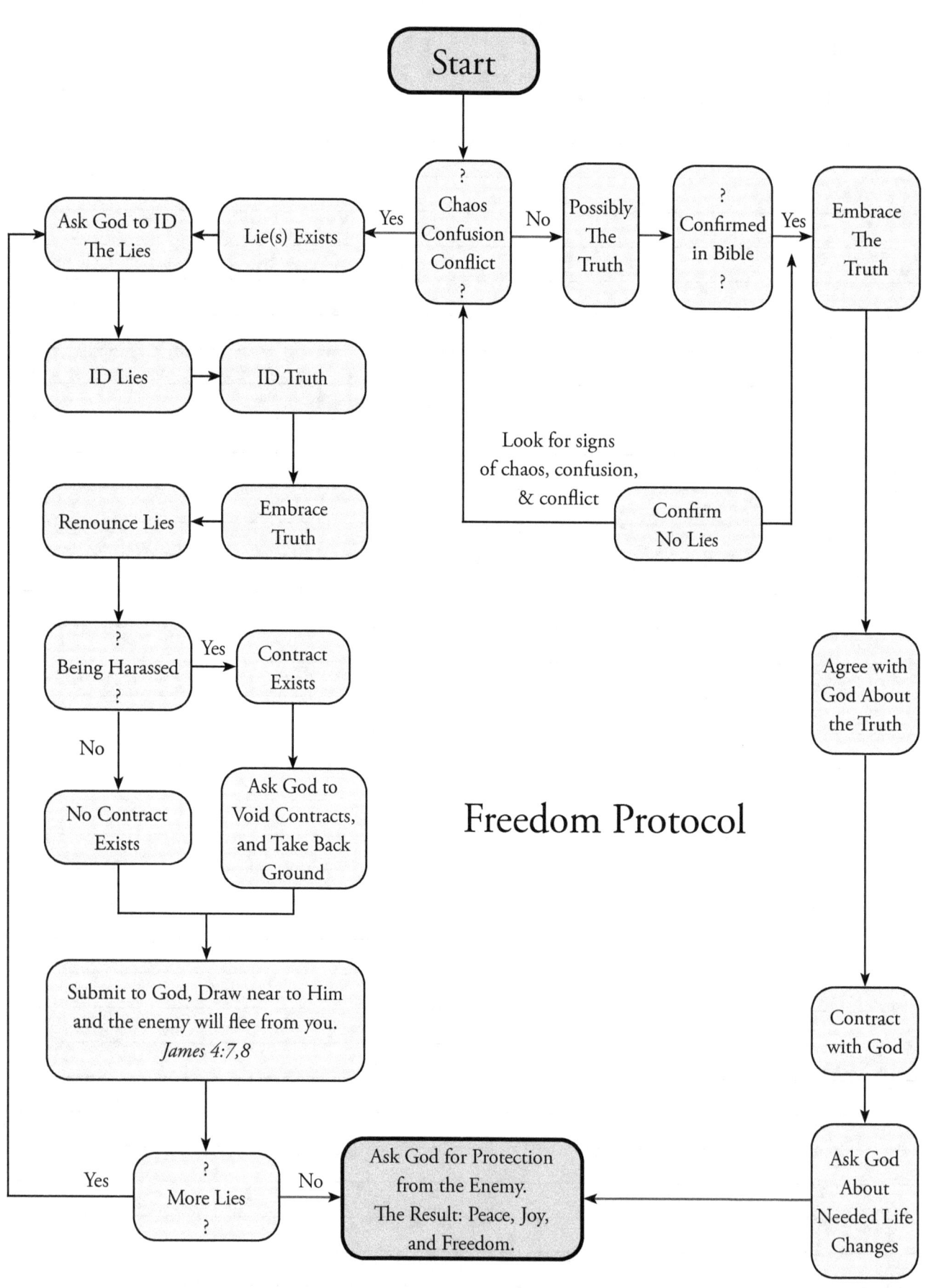

Chapter Two:

Freedom Protocol

The Freedom Protocol flow chart to the left shows in detail the steps you can take to experience freedom from the enemy.

1. Does the Freedom Protocol flow chart make sense? Any thoughts?
   _____
   _____
   _____
   _____

2. Which part of the Freedom Protocol do you perceive to be the most difficult?
   _____
   _____
   _____
   _____

3. Does the idea of *predictable* results in the Christian life appeal to you?
   _____
   _____

4. Definition of **Protocol**:

   "A proven procedure or system of rules by which one can achieve a desired and measurable result or outcome."

   In our context, the protocols define the rules by which we interact with the enemy. Knowing these protocols will help the reader to be delivered from the power of sin.

5. Definition of **Remedy**:

   "A means of counteracting or eliminating something undesirable."

   In our context, the remedies described herein are provided by God to deliver us from the power of sin. These remedies are relied upon by us as we address the defined protocols. God has provided a number of

> *What if a change in our thinking, could give us more victory in our lives?*
>
> *What if we could be less harassed and tormented by the enemy, and/or not controlled by our addic-tions or the enemy's temp-tations?*

remedies (deliverances) to rescue us from the power of sin. The remedies are what we exercise to get relief from an undesirable circumstance.

6. Definition of **Salvation**:

    "A preservation or deliverance from harm, ruin, or loss caused by sin and the enemy of our souls."

In our context, this is the plan devised by God to weed out and destroy sin and to restore us to Himself.

7. Who is responsible for you discovering truth?

_____
_____
_____
_____
_____

> *"When the Spirit of truth comes, he will guide you into all truth. He will not speak on his own but will tell you what he has heard. He will tell you about the future."*
>
> John 16:13
>
> *"Whether you turn to the right or to the left, your ears will hear a voice behind you, saying, 'This is the way; walk in it.'"*
>
> Isaiah 30:21

8. What is the difference between power and authority?

_____
_____
_____
_____

9. Does a different payer life with God interest you?

_____
_____
_____
_____

10. Do you love the truth? Read II Thessalonians 2:5-12

_____
_____
_____
_____
_____
_____

11. At what cost? Have you experienced the cost of embracing the truth?

12. With a personal temptation (or two) in mind, can you see how following this protocol can help you have victory over sin and the enemy? If not, why?

13. Is the above Freedom Protocol a process anyone can use regardless of how mature they might be in their relationship with God? If not, why?

14. Is it encouraging to know that there is a proven remedy to overcome the enemy's temptations?

15. Does having a remedy affect any attitudes you might have about God?

> *Definition Remedy:*
>
> *"A means of counteracting or eliminating something undesirable."*

16. Pick one issue in your life with chaos, confusion, and/or conflict. Describe your experience using the Freedom Protocol on that personal issue:

___

Notes:

For your thoughts, insights, and questions . . .

Chapter Three:

Temptation and the Rules of Engagement

1. What was your first reaction to reading about the *Rules of Engagement* in chapter 3 of the book?

   _____
   _____
   _____

> *Definition Rule of Engagement:*
>
> *"A directive issued by a military authority specifying the circumstances and limitations under which forces will engage in combat with the enemy."*

2. Were you surprised to learn that "lawless" prisoners follow their own rules to regulate their interactions with each other?

   _____
   _____
   _____
   _____

3. Is it encouraging to know that God, the author of law, has rules of engagement to help you overcome the enemy's temptations?

   _____
   _____
   _____
   _____
   _____

4. What are your thoughts about the Temptation Protocol below? Does it encourage you? Why?

___

"No temptation has overtaken you except what is common to mankind.
And God is faithful; he will not let [permission] you be tempted beyond what you can bear.
But when you are tempted, he will also provide <u>a way out</u> [limitations]
so that you can endure it." I Cor. 10:13

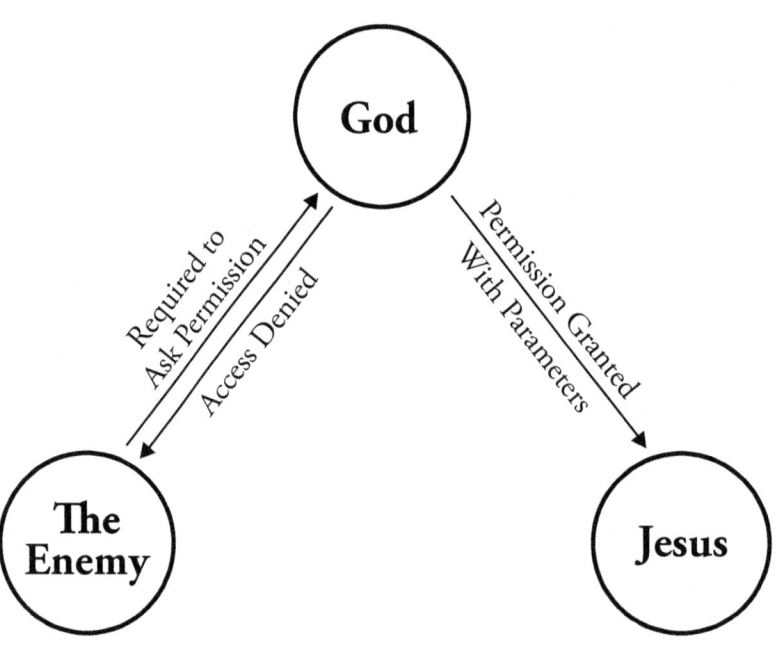

Figure 1

5. Is the Temptation Protocol consistent with Paul's encouragement in *I Corinthians 10:13*? Why?

___

CHAPTER 3: TEMPTATION AND THE RULES OF ENGAGEMENT

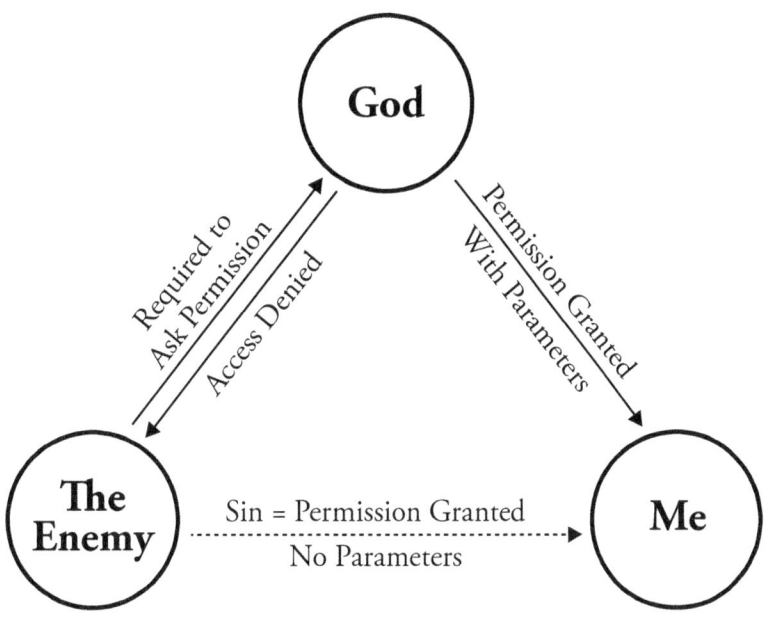

Figure 2

6. Does the temptation protocol above explain why sin can be overwhelming at times?

_____
_____
_____

7. How did John grant the enemy access to his life?

_____
_____
_____
_____
_____
_____
_____
_____
_____
_____
_____

> *John's Story*
>
> *John, a traveling salesman was addicted to pornography for over fifteen years. He often asked God to take his addiction away. Every time he was tempted, he resisted for a while but would later give in leading to discouragement and depression. By exercising these protocols, in a matter of a few hours, John specifically renounced the access he had granted the enemy to his life. He felt free and clean for the first time. Three weeks later, John called exclaiming "Joe, I just realized this morning that I have not had a single pornographic thought in three weeks!"*

8. When I grant the enemy access to my life by sinning, what are God's lawful rights with respect to the permission I granted the enemy?

___

9. Was John's request that God take away his desire for pornography lawful or lawless? Why?

___

10. What do you think goes through the heart of God when we ask Him to act unlawfully or unjustly?

___

11. Why do you think John had no pornographic thoughts for three weeks.?

___

12. Did God regulate the enemy's access to Adam and Eve in the Garden of Eden? If so, how did He do so?
   _____
   _____
   _____
   _____
   _____

   > *See the Bible account of the Adam and Eve in the Garden of Eden.*
   >
   > *Genesis 3*

   > *Is there any Scriptural conflict with the Temptation Protocol as presented here?*

13. Do you think there are any problems with the temptation protocols? If so, please explain:
   _____
   _____
   _____
   _____
   _____
   _____
   _____
   _____
   _____
   _____
   _____
   _____
   _____
   _____
   _____
   _____
   _____
   _____
   _____
   _____
   _____

Notes:

For your thoughts, insights, and questions . . .

Chapter Four:

Truth and Lies

1. Are you convinced that God is truth and the enemy is falsehood?
   _____
   _____
   _____
   _____
   _____
   _____
   _____

2. Is the following true? See book, pg. 42.
   - Every time we sin it is because we believe a lie of the enemy.
   - When we believe a lie of the enemy it leads to sin.
   - Even if we believe a lie of the enemy about the truth it leads to sin.
   - It is impossible for us to sin by believing the truth.
   - Can you think of any exceptions?

   _____
   _____
   _____
   _____
   _____
   _____

> *Does God always present Himself in Scripture as being perfectly just?*

3. Is there a crisis of belief each time we are faced with the enemy's lies and the truth of God?

4. Does it help you to know that the truth Jesus is referring to is not just about theology or doctrine but any issue in our life?

5. What did you think about Gary's story and obedience? See book, pg. 45

Notes:

For your thoughts, insights, and questions . . .

Chapter Five:

Contracts

1. Are all agreements in fact contracts?
   _____
   _____

2. Have you ever considered the idea that when you agree with the enemy's lies, you are contracting with him?
   _____
   _____
   _____

Contract Element	Meaning Within Law	Meaning Regarding Temptation
Offer	Proposition made by the Offeror	Temptation wrapped in a lie made by the Enemy
Acceptance	Agreement with the Offeror. Generally, by means of a signature.	Agreement with the Enemy's lie. Achieved by our actions which reveal our agreement.
Consideration	A desired outcome or the hope of a desired outcome	A promise of, what appears to be, a desired outcome. Seldom is the consideration fully realized.
Obligation	Each party is bound to perform according to the proposition and desired outcome. If a written contract, a signature is required. If unwritten, actions are required.	The Enemy binds us to performance to the offer we accepted. Since our contracts with the Enemy are unwritten, it is our actions that bind us to the contract.
Competency and Capacity	Each party has the lawful capacity to be held to a particular performance. Minors lack the competency to be bound to a contract.	The Enemy lies by promising what he cannot accomplish.

Table 1

3. From Table #1 above, are all the elements of a contract present when we agree with the enemy's lies?

4. Are contracts binding?

5. Have you ever tried to get out of a contract? Explain.

6. Is there any example in Scripture where God allows the enemy unrestrained access to our lives, without parameters?

7. Does the marriage example in Chapter 5, pg. 56 of the book make sense and do you see it as applicable to breaking contracts with the enemy?

8. Is it encouraging to know that the remedy to break every contract we have with the enemy is built into every temptation and sin?

9. Do you have any thoughts about Fred's story on pg. 57 of the book?

Notes:

For your thoughts, insights, and questions . . .

	#	Remedies	Meaning of Remedies
S A L V A T I O N	1	Deliverance from the **Pollution** of Sin	This deliverance occurs when we receive Jesus as Lord and Savior. Receiving Him means we have eternal life in Jesus and no matter how sinful our past, we are cleansed in a moment of all our sin. (I John 1:7; I John 5:11-12)
	2	Deliverance from the **Power** of Sin	This deliverance occurs between the time we receive Jesus as Lord and the second coming of Jesus. This is the time when God expects us to be overcomers and to rule over sin. (Rom. 8:2)
	3	Deliverance from the **Presence** of Sin	At Jesus' second coming He saves the righteous and removes them from the very presence of sin. (John 14:1-3)
	4	Deliverance from the **Propensity** to Sin	Also at Jesus' return, those still living on the earth, who have struggled with their sinful nature for so many years, are changed in a moment and are delivered from their sinful nature and propensity to sin. (I Cor. 15:52)
	5	Deliverance from the **Pronouncement** of Sin	After the second coming and the thousand-year millennium, there is the great white throne judgment where the wicked are judged and publicly pronounced guilty of sin and sentenced to the penalty of second death in the lake of fire. (Rev. 20:11)
	6	Deliverance from the **Penalty** of Sin	Following the judgment, the wicked receive the penalty for sin. They are destroyed and perish in the lake of fire. This is the second death. The wages of sin is death. (Rev. 21:8, Rom. 6:23)
	7	Deliverance from the **Possibility** of Sin	After the wicked are punished and destroyed, God creates a new heaven and a new earth where all traces of sin have been eliminated from God's universe, and there is no possibility of sin ever returning again. (I Thess. 5:23)

Table 2

Chapter Six:

Ruling Over Sin

1. Based on table 2, pg. 62 in the book, is Salvation more involved than you previously thought? Explain:

2. What is the difference between Salvation and Deliverance?

3. How does this affect your view of God?

4. What are your thoughts about ruling over sin?

5. When it comes to dealing with sin, what is God's expectation for us? See Genesis 4:6-7.

6. Are God's Expectations Just?

7. Are God's Expectations Loving?

8. As a principle of law and justice, can God be just and at the same time make a law that cannot be kept?

CHAPTER 6: RULING OVER SIN

9. Since it is unlawful to create a law which cannot be kept, does this affect your previous thoughts about keeping God's commands?

10. How can God's expectation that we rule over sin be compatible with our sinful nature and weakness?

11. Could a different understanding as to *what is sin* help us understand God's expectations that we rule over sin?

Notes:

For your thoughts, insights, and questions . . .

Chapter Seven:

What is Sin?

1. Considering the Freedom Protocols, what do you think about God's expectation that we rule over sin?

   _____
   _____
   _____
   _____
   _____
   _____
   _____

2. Can you think of any Biblical example of one who was punished only because of their sinful nature?

   _____
   _____
   _____
   _____
   _____
   _____
   _____

3. Can you think of any Biblical example of one who was punished only because of their intent to sin without an associated action?

   _____
   _____
   _____
   _____

4. Does sin as a combination of both *Actus Reus* (actions) and *Mens Rea* (intent) conflict with Scripture?

5. Does the concept of sin being both action and intent as presented in chapter 7 of the book affect your thinking relative to God's expectation that we rule over sin?

6. Does the formula of Evil Actions + Evil Intent = Sin help you understand Romans 7:14-20?

7. Do you have a different view of the tenth commandment now? See book, pg. 77.

CHAPTER 7: WHAT IS SIN?

8. What do you think about Rusdoony's observations?

    "Thus what is clearly condemned by the tenth commandment is every attempt to gain by fraud, coercion, or deceit that which belongs to our neighbor. On this principle, alienation of affection suits were once a part of the law of the land. Their abuse by a lawless age led to their abolition, but the principle is sound. A person who works systematically to alienate the affections of a husband or wife in order to gain him or her for himself, sometimes together with his monetary assets, is guilty of violating this law."

    _____
    _____
    _____
    _____
    _____
    _____

9. In Eve's case study, can you identify the moment when Eve actually sinned? See book, pg. 83, 84

    - "the woman saw that the fruit of the tree was good for food.
    - "and pleasing to the eye,
    - "and also desirable for gaining wisdom,
    - "she took some and ate it."

    _____
    _____
    _____
    _____
    _____
    _____

10. Does the following Scripture make more or less sense after reading this chapter?

    "Now what I am commanding you today is not too difficult for you or beyond your reach."
    Deuteronomy 30:11

    _____
    _____
    _____
    _____
    _____
    _____

Notes:

For your thoughts, insights, and questions . . .

Chapter Eight:

Only by God's Authority

1. Have you felt in the past that it was easier to live in the kingdom of darkness than the kingdom of light?
   _____
   _____
   _____
   _____
   _____
   _____

Figure 3

2. Is it encouraging to know that for every contract we have with the enemy, the remedy for that contract is built into every temptation and sin?
   _____
   _____
   _____
   _____
   _____
   _____

3. When you read the following steps to victory, what is your first reaction?
   - Discover the lies and resulting contracts we have established with the enemy.
   - Lawfully renounce the contracts based on the lies upon which they are based.
   - Ask God to lawfully void the contracts because they are based on the lies.
   - Establish a new contract with God based on the truth He has revealed to you.
   - Ask God to lawfully protect His property rights in accordance with the temptation protocol of permission and parameters.

   _____
   _____
   _____
   _____
   _____

When you read John 8:32, how would you answer questions 4 and 5 below?

> *"To the Jews who had believed him, Jesus said, "If you hold to my teaching, you are really my disciples. Then you will know the truth, and the truth will set you free." John 8:31,32*

4. What is the truth that you need to know to be free?

   _____
   _____
   _____
   _____
   _____

5. When you know that truth, from what does it set you free?

   _____
   _____
   _____
   _____
   _____

> *"But when he, the Spirit of truth, comes, he will guide you into all the truth." John 16:13*

6. Does John 16:13 help us know who is responsible to teach you the truth?

   _____
   _____
   _____

CHAPTER 8: ONLY BY GOD'S AUTHORITY

7. Do you believe that the truth about anything will set you free from those lies of the enemy?

8. Does the truth seem like an effective way to rule over sin?

Kingdom Of Darkness (Lies) — **Kingdom Of Light (Truth)**

Figure 4

9. Does using truth against the enemy give you a different view of the two kingdoms and your relationship to them?

10. Can you think of any other reasons why God would allow the enemy to tempt us?

11. Can you think of times you have asked God to act unlawfully on your behalf?

12. Is it encouraging to know that we all have the same access to God's authority and deliverance regardless of our Christian maturity?

13. What are your thoughts about Kalini's experience on pg. 95 of the book?

Notes:

For your thoughts, insights, and questions . . .

Chapter Nine:

Identifying the Lies

1. What is the difference between Circumstantial and Foundational lies?
   _____
   _____
   _____
   _____
   _____

2. Was it easy to tell the difference between the Circumstantial and Foundational lies you have believed?
   _____
   _____
   _____
   _____
   _____

3. Ask God to reveal two Foundational lies you have believed? List them below.
   _____
   _____
   _____
   _____

4. Thinking about this past week, can you identify the footprints of the enemy and of Jesus? Can you give an example?
   _____
   _____
   _____
   _____
   _____

5. What do you think about relationship and isolation as it relates to God and the enemy?

_____
_____
_____
_____
_____
_____
_____
_____

> *You shall know the truth and the truth shall set you free.*

6. Did the Greek and Hebrew meaning of "Repentance" affect your thinking about Repentance?

_____
_____
_____
_____
_____

7. Can you identify any lies you have believed that require a change in your thinking (Repentance)?

_____
_____
_____
_____
_____
_____
_____
_____

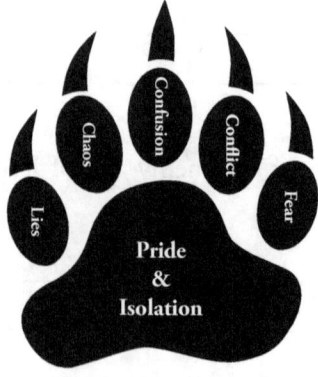

FIGURE 5
The enemy's footprint.

FIGURE 6
Jesus' footprint

Notes:

For your thoughts, insights, and questions . . .

Chapter Ten:

Forgiveness

> *When you apologize for your actions and you are forgiven, the pain you caused may remain; but*
>
> *When you apologize for the pain you caused, and you are forgiven, you are completely forgiven for both the pain you caused and the action.*

1. What are your thoughts about "Apology 101" on page 118 of the book?

   _____
   _____
   _____
   _____
   _____

2. Have you tried making an apology for the pain you caused? What was the response you received?

   _____
   _____
   _____
   _____
   _____
   _____
   _____

> *When we forgive another for their actions, the pain they caused can remain; but*
>
> *When we forgive another for the pain they caused, they are automatically forgiven for both the action and the pain they caused.*

3. What are your thoughts on the rules for forgiving from the heart? See Matthew 18:21:35
_____
_____
_____
_____
_____

4. List some of the enemy's lies you have heard about forgiveness.
_____
_____
_____
_____
_____

> *"For if, while we were God's enemies, we were reconciled to him through the death of his Son, how much more, <u>having been reconciled</u> [past tense], shall we be saved through his life!" Romans 5:10*

5. Why is it important that forgiveness does not require anything from the offending party?
_____
_____
_____
_____
_____
_____
_____

6. Does God forgive in the same way that He asks us to forgive?
_____
_____
_____
_____
_____

7. What stood out to you when you read the parable of the unjust servant in Matthew 18:23-35?
_____
_____
_____
_____
_____

8. Does Jesus treat forgiveness as a serious matter?

_____
_____
_____
_____
_____

Note: The exercise below is a sample of what will be explained in more detail in the next section and final chapters. In the next section and chapters, you will more fully exercise what you have learned thus far. If you have any questions, remember to email us at info@h4hm.org and we will be happy to answer your questions.

9. **Exercise** - Pick someone who has deeply wounded you and work through that person's actions towards you and forgive them using the forms found at the end of this workbook or at: https://www.h4hm.org/book-resources
   Look for the following forms:
   - People Who Have Wounded Me.
   - Emotional Pain Words.

   You will need the Emotional Pain Words form for the last column of the People Who Have Wounded Me form.

10. Review Chapter 10 of the book, starting at pg. 111.

11. As you get started with this exercise, know that the enemy of your soul does not want you to get free of bitterness. He will say things like:
    - You have already forgiven that person.
    - This is too difficult, and it will be too painful for you.
    - It won't help you to bring up the past again. It's best to move on and ignore those people who have wounded you.
    - Give yourself a couple of days to think about this and don't start the inventory list right away.

12. Be committed to getting this list done and prayed through. Freedom is awaiting you on the other side of this exercise.

13. Take your time. Do not be anxious. Just let the Holy Spirit speak to your mind and heart. This cannot be forced. Focus on the journey not the destination.

> *Tips*
>
> *As you do the forgiveness exercise, pick just one or two events to start. Later, you can address other actions they have done.*
>
> *As you forgive, focus on forgiving that person for the pain they caused you.*
>
> *Pay attention to the lies of the enemy as you work through this forgiveness process and renounce the lies and embrace the truth as revealed in God's word regarding that lie.*

14. When you are ready to start praying through the list, find a quiet place where you will not be disturbed, turn off your cell phone, and pray. In an unrushed manner, acknowledge, renounce, and repent of each bitterness stronghold/contract on your inventory list. Here is a sample prayer:

"Lord I choose to forgive_____(Name)_____ for _____(The way I was wounded)_____, causing me to feel _____(the emotional pain I felt)_____. I am willing to pay for the emotional pain and consequences that _____(Name)_____ caused me. I ask you, Jesus, to break and void all of Satan's strongholds and contracts in my life caused by my bitterness. I take back the ground I gave to Satan by my bitterness, and I yield that ground to You."

You may want to refer to Chapter 10 of the book to better understand each element of the above prayer.

When you are finished with the entire list, talk to God about it. You may find these steps helpful as you completely forgive this person:

Pray—

1. "Lord, I am done with bitterness and the enemy's lies regarding my bitterness."

2. "Are there any remaining bitterness issues You want to talk to me about?"

3. If more events related to bitterness and lies are revealed to you, jot them down on the list. Pray through that newly revealed event that needs to be forgiven. Return to Step 2 to determine if there is any other bitterness the Lord wants to talk to you about. If there is nothing else to address, go to Step 4.

4. When nothing more is revealed, ask God to show you in some way that you are free and clean of all the bitterness/strongholds/contracts regarding the bitterness you prayed through. He may show or tell you that you are clean and free by revealing to you one or more of the following: a song, picture (video), scripture verse, or quotation.

5. This will be meaningful to you specifically and will not be repeated with anyone else you may try to help in this way.

6. If nothing happens when you work through Step 4, be patient. Often you may be prompted later when it is unexpected. God is incredibly creative, and He will connect with you in a special way that will bless you more than you could ever imagine.

7. **Note:** You can add other names and events to another sheet and forgive those individuals as well. This should now be a lifestyle. As soon as you discover someone who needs to be forgiven, take the form, add their name, event and pain words and work through each of them until you are done.

CHAPTER 10: FORGIVENESS

15. Share what God did for you as you forgave each person from your heart.

16. Be sure to jot down what God shows you during your prayer time so you can recall that moment when God told you that you were clean and free of bitterness. When the enemy tries to remind you of the past, remind him that these strongholds/contracts are void back to the beginning. Then ask God to intervene to protect you and the contract you made with Him since you now believe and embrace the truth. It might also be helpful to remind the enemy of his future!

Notes:

For your thoughts, insights, and questions . . .

PART 2:

Practical Applications

Chapter Eleven:

Let's Get Started

1. Ask God for His help as you begin to look at the lies in your life.

    "Lord, I acknowledge that I have sinned and given the enemy access to and authority in my life by believing his lies. As I begin, give me discernment regarding the Truth about any chaos, confusion and conflict in my life and the enemy's lies. As I renounce his lies, I ask You to break and void the enemy's strongholds and contracts in my life. I ask You to void the access and authority I gave to the enemy by believing his lies and I return that access and authority to You. Watch over my heart and continue to teach me the truth that will set me free. In Jesus' Name, Amen."

2. Pick two difficulties in life on which you want to focus. Try to pick a couple of things that are significant. Remember that you are looking to resolve a constant source of harassment.

    _____
    _____
    _____
    _____
    _____
    _____
    _____
    _____

> *Remember that your life with God is a journey and not a trip. Take your time and rest in and embrace the work that God is doing in your heart and life in the moment.*
>
> *Often a spouse or good friend can help you identify issues that are significant to you.*

3. Copy from the back of the workbook or download and print several copies of the Breaking Strongholds document using your web browser: https://www.h4hm.org/book-resources

4. As you begin, ask God again for specific help. Remember that He is a vital part of this work you are doing. You can't do this alone.

> *Dear Lord, I want to be free and I acknowledge that I have believed lies of the enemy for far too long. Please help me discover the enemy's lies in my life and help me discern the truth that will set me free. I trust you to give me just what I can handle. Send Your Holy Spirit to speak truth into my heart and life. Amen.*

5. Enter the difficulty you want to address in the first column. For example, "Self-esteem," "Anger," etc.

Sin/Strongholds/Contracts	The Enemy's Lies which you have believed
Self-esteem	

6. In the second column, enter the lies you have believed regarding identified issue.

Sin/Strongholds/Contracts	The Enemy's Lies which you have believed
Self-esteem	*There is something wrong with me.*
	I'm stupid.
	No one likes me.

7. It will be helpful to decide if this is a Circumstantial lie or a Foundational lie you have believed for many years. See book, pg. 138.

8. What is the truth regarding each of the lies above?

C/F	God's Truth as revealed by His Spirit or His Word
F	*No one is perfect. God loves me as I am.*
F	*Stupid is a feeling. I'm clever lots of times.*
F	*I have friends. I can make more friends.*
F	

9. After you have made a list of lies and truth for the one issue you have identified, pray through each lie and truth using this prayer:

"Lord I acknowledge and renounce the enemy's lie that ___(The Lie)___ by which I granted the enemy access to and authority in my life. I renounce that lie and I ask You to void that lie-filled contract of the enemy to which I agreed by believing his lies. I choose to believe the Truth that ___(The Truth)___. I take back the access and authority to my heart I gave to the enemy by believing his lie, and I return that access and authority to You. Jesus, set my heart free according to your promise. I ask you to stand at the door of my heart and protect me from the enemy's temptations and lies."

10. When you are done, ask God if you missed any lies. If you see additional lies, work through them as you did in chapter 10 #9 above.

    Remember the following:
    - It is the truth that sets you free, not identifying the lies.
    - It is God who voids the contracts not you.
    - Don't fret over the lies, ust resolve them when the Holy Spirit reveals them to you each day.
    - Review the Scripture verses at the end of Chapter 11.
    - Thank God daily for setting you free from these contracts.

> *If you so choose, you can pick up these lies again and you will come under contract and harassment again. You are free to choose bondage again. Praise and thanksgiving are the best ways to stay free over time.*

11. How did God reveal to you that the bondage and contracts were voided?

___
___
___
___
___
___
___
___
___
___
___
___
___
___
___
___
___
___
___
___

Notes:

For your thoughts, insights, and questions . . .

Chapter Twelve:

Pride and Humility

1. How does the idea of Happiness and Humility being a by-product strike you?
   _____
   _____
   _____

> *"Humble yourselves, therefore, under God's mighty hand, so that in due time He may exalt you."*
> *I Peter 5:6*
>
> *"Humble yourselves before the Lord, and He will exalt you."*
> *James 4:10*

2. In your experience, does the relationship between believing the enemy's lies and pride hold true?
   _____
   _____
   _____

3. When you are experiencing chaos, confusion and conflict, are pride and lies in the middle of those experiences?
   _____
   _____
   _____
   _____

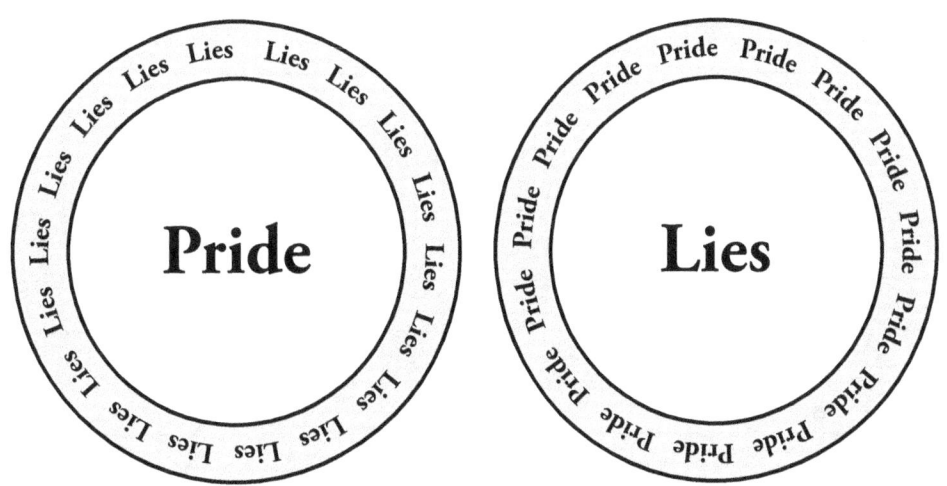

4. Can you think of any lie of the enemy that will cause you to be humble?

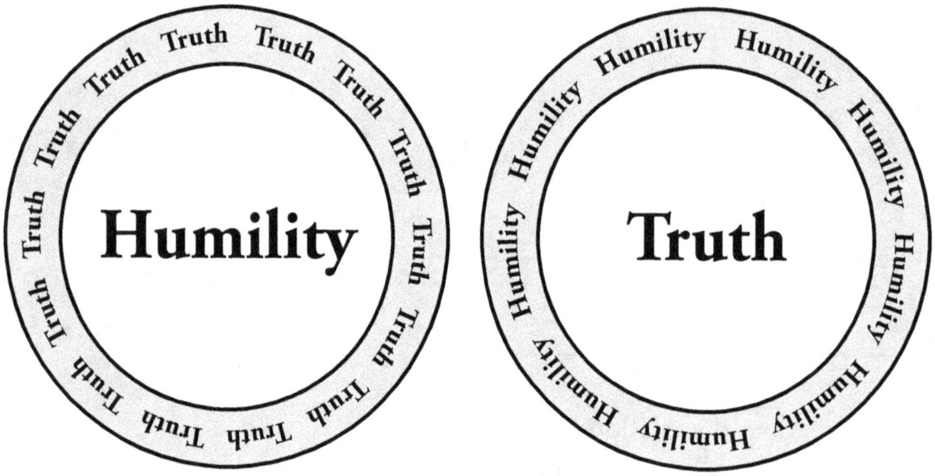

5. When you believe and embrace the truth, do you experience peace, and do you find yourself teachable?

6. Can you think of any truth of God that will cause you to be prideful?

7. When you feel like you must defend yourself, does that come from pride or humility?

8. Who is responsible for and has a vested interest in your reputation?

9. How do you feel about trusting God with your reputation?

10. My action plan to renounce pride and embrace humility:

Notes:

For your thoughts, insights, and questions . . .

Chapter Thirteen:

Hardship and Trials

What are the answers to the following questions?

1. Is God perfectly just at all times?

2. Is God redemptive in all that He does?

3. Will God always do what is best for you? If yes, on what basis are you convinced that He will always do what is best for you?

4. Are you satisfied that hardship is a blessing? If so, why?

5. What is the difference between hardship and temptation?

6. Can you identify times in your life when you were blessed by God and His blessing was snatched away by the enemy?

7. When you experience chaos, confusion and conflict, are you focused on the past, present or the now?

> *The only trees at which people throw rocks are the ones with fruit.*

8. How does the statement on the left make you feel about being fruitful?

9. Did God forsake the martyrs of the Christian faith?

10. What are some of the lies the enemy tells us about hardship?

Notes:

For your thoughts, insights, and questions . . .

Chapter Fourteen:

Vigilance and Perseverance

1. How does C. S. Lewis' statement at the right strike you?

> *"It would seem that our Lord finds our desires not too strong, but too weak. We are half-hearted creatures, fooling about with drink and sex and ambition when infinite joy is offered us, like an ignorant child who wants to go on making mud pies in a slum because he cannot imagine what is meant by the offer of a holiday at the sea. We are far too easily pleased."*
>
> *C. S. Lewis*

2. Do you find that you often trade the joy God promises you for the "happiness" you know?

3. Is there a way to be vigilant without white-knuckling our way through life?

4. Does a spirit of thankfulness really keep you free?

5. If the truth often hurts, why would we want to embrace the truth?

6. Can exercising the protocols and remedies become mechanical?

7. Is it possible to lose sight of the Savior as I make the effort to rule over sin in my life?

8. How can I remind myself that ruling over sin is accomplished when I rely on God's authority and not my own strength?

9. This is my plan to rule over sin in my life starting today.

Notes:

For your thoughts, insights, and questions . . .

Chapter Fifteen:

Is Jesus Necessary?

1. When you read in Isaiah 14:12-15 how Satan wants to put his throne above that of God, how did that strike you?
   _____
   _____
   _____
   _____
   _____
   _____

2. Do you think that Satan's attitude reflects on the way God rules over His kingdom?
   _____
   _____
   _____
   _____
   _____
   _____

> *"How you are fallen from heaven, O Day Star, son of Dawn! How you are cut down to the ground, you who laid the nations low! You said in your heart, I will ascend to heaven; above the stars of God I will set my throne on high; I will sit on the mount of assembly in the far reaches of the north;"*
> Isaiah 14:12-15

3. How do you feel about God taking the punishment His justice demands upon Himself in the person of Jesus?
   _____
   _____
   _____
   _____
   _____

> *God presented Christ as a sacrifice of atonement through the shedding of his blood—to be received by faith. He did this to demonstrate his righteousness, because in his forbearance he had left the sins committed beforehand unpunished— 26 he did it to demonstrate his righteousness at the present time, so as to be just and the one who justifies those who have faith in Jesus. Romans 3:25-26*

4. Does God taking the demands of His justice upon himself affect your thinking about Who God is?

_____
_____
_____
_____
_____
_____
_____

5. Is there anything stopping you from embracing and trusting in the truth of Jesus today?

_____
_____
_____
_____
_____
_____
_____
_____
_____
_____

6. Would you share what exercising the protocols has done for you?

_____
_____
_____
_____
_____

7. Would you share your experience of receiving Jesus?

_____
_____
_____
_____
_____
_____

Notes:

For your thoughts, insights, and questions . . .

Lastly

Tell Us Your Experiences

This book was written for your success. The protocols work for any issue in which you find yourself being harassed and tormented by the enemy, such as immorality, pride, hypocrisy, addictions, anger, profanity, rebellion, low self-esteem, impatience, and greed. Please let us know how you are doing as you implement the protocols and how we can make this book more effective for you and others. If you get stuck somewhere in the process, let us know what was difficult for you to understand or to implement.

Hearing about your difficulties will help us make the book and this workbook easier to understand for someone else. There is a Forum at https://www.h4hm.org where you can share your experiences with others. Be courteous with those who are struggling and may be having difficulty getting their arms around these protocols. As we share our experiences, we are confident that you will discover that these protocols and remedies will be applicable to other issues in your life we may not have covered here. We look forward to hearing from you as you apply these principles in your life. You can also email us anytime at info@h4hm.org.

May the Lord bless you in this new and exciting adventure of your life.

Acknowledgement

My Bible Study class studied this book over 15 weeks and they were a huge influence in helping discover ways to adjust the book and this workbook to work in a weekly Bible study context. I am so grateful for these class members who are students of God's word and who are not afraid to push back when they have difficulty understanding the issues presented here and in the book.

APPENDIX:

Forms

Breaking Enemy Strongholds

Name: _____ Date: _____ Page: _____

*1. Identify the besetting/habitual sin(s) in your life, 2. Identify The enemy's lie(s) believed regarding that sin, 3. Mark the lie(s) as **F**oundational or **C**ircumstantial, and 4. Identify the truth(s) regarding the enemy's lies as revealed by God's Word or by His Spirit. Ask for God's discernment to see the lie(s) and to know the Truth.*

Prayer: *"Lord, I acknowledge that I have sinned and given the enemy access to and authority in my life by believing his lies. As I begin, give me discernment regarding the enemy's lies and the truth about my sin and his lies. As I renounce the enemy's lies, I ask You to break and void all his strongholds and contracts in my life. I also ask You to take back the access and authority I once gave to the enemy by believing his lies. I choose now to return that access and authority to You. Watch over my heart and continue to teach me the truth that will remain free. In Jesus' Name, Amen."*.

Sin/Strongholds/Contracts	The Enemy's Lies which you have believed	C/F	God's Truth as revealed by His Spirit or His Word
•	•		

"Lord, I acknowledge and renounce the enemy's lie that ____(The Lie).____ by which I granted the enemy access to and authority in my life. I renounce that lie and I ask You to void that lie-filled contract of the enemy to which I agreed by believing his lies. I choose to believe the Truth that ____(The truth)____. I take back the access and authority to my heart I gave to the enemy by believing his lie, and I return that access and authority to You. Jesus, set my heart free according to Your promise. I ask You to stand at the door of my heart and protect me from the enemy's temptations and lies."

APPENDIX: FORMS

Sin/Strongholds/Contracts	The Enemy's Lies which you have believed	C/F	God's Truth as revealed by His Spirit or His Word
•	•		

"Lord I acknowledge and renounce the enemy's lie that ____(The Lie)____ by which I granted the enemy access to and authority in my life. I renounce that lie and I ask You to void that lie-filled contract of the enemy to which I agreed by believing his lies. I choose to believe the Truth that ____(The Truth)____. I take back the access and authority to my heart I gave to the enemy by believing his lie, and I return that access and authority to You. Jesus, set my heart free according to your promise. I ask you to stand at the door of my heart and protect me from the enemy's temptations and lies."

People Who Have Wounded Me

Name: _____ Date: _____ Page: _____

- Father (Bio/Step)
- Mother (Bio/Step)
- Grandparents
- Other family members
- Siblings
- Friends
- Teachers/Students/Class Experiences
- Employer/employees
- Believers/church situations
- Others
- God/Ways God has hurt you
- Yourself

List individuals who have wounded you (Use first names if possible to identify)	How they wounded you (List issues and events)	Describe the emotional pain you felt (List **5 or 6** Emotional pain words for each)
•	•	

"Lord, I choose to forgive _____(Name)_____ for _____(The way I was wounded)_____, causing me to feel _____(The emotional pain I felt)_____. I am willing to pay for the emotional pain and consequences that _____(Name)_____ caused me. I ask you, Jesus, to break and void all of Satan's strongholds and contracts in my life caused by my bitterness. I take back the ground I gave to Satan by my bitterness, and I yield that ground to You."

© Joseph Saladino -- 2022

H4HM-05.6.0-People-Who-Have-Wounded-Me.docx

APPENDIX: FORMS

List individuals who wounded you (Use first names if possible to identify)	How they wounded you (List issues and events)	Describe the emotional pain you felt (List 5 or 6 Emotional pain words for each)
•	•	

"Lord, I choose to forgive _____(Name)_____ for _____(The way I was wounded)_____, causing me to feel ___(The emotional pain I felt)___. I am willing to pay for the emotional pain and consequences that _____(Name)_____ caused me. I ask you, Jesus, to break and void all of Satan's strongholds and contracts in my life caused by my bitterness. I take back the ground I gave to Satan by my bitterness, and I yield that ground to You."

Emotional Pain Words

Instructions: Evaluate each word on the basis of 0 to 5 (0=not significant, 5=very significant). On the left side of each word mark ONLY the words which you determine to be a 3, 4, or 5. If you see a word that seems to jump off the page when you see it, circle that word (there should only be 1 or 2 of these words). Add other missing words at the end.

___ Abandoned	___ Didn't measure up	___ Left out	___ Suffocated
___ Accused	___ Dirty	___ Lied to	___ Suicidal
___ Afraid	___ Disappointed	___ Lonely	___ Taken advantage of
___ All my fault	___ Disconnected	___ Lost	___ Terrified
___ Alone	___ Discounted	___ Made fun of	___ Thwarted
___ Always wrong	___ Discouraged	___ Manipulated	___ Torn apart
___ Angry	___ Disgusted	___ Mindless	___ Trapped
___ Anxious	___ Disheartened	___ Mistreated	___ Trash
___ Apathetic	___ Disrespected	___ Misunderstood	___ Ugly
___ Ashamed	___ Dominated	___ Molested	___ Unable to communicate
___ Avoided	___ Done	___ Neglected	___ Unaccepted
___ Awkward	___ Embarrassed	___ No good	___ Uncaring
___ Babied	___ Empty	___ Not being affirmed	___ Uncared for
___ Bad	___ Exhausted	___ Not cared for	___ Unchosen
___ Belittled	___ Exposed	___ Not cherished	___ Unclean
___ Betrayal	___ Failure	___ Not deserving to live	___ Unconnected
___ Betrayed	___ Fear, Fearful	___ Not good enough	___ Unfairly judged
___ Bewildered	___ Foolish	___ Not listened to	___ Unfairly treated
___ Bitter	___ Forced	___ Not measure up	___ Unfit
___ Blamed	___ Frightened	___ Not valued	___ Unheard
___ Bullied	___ Frozen	___ Numb	___ Unimportant
___ Burdened	___ Frustrated	___ Obligated	___ Unknown
___ Can't do anything right	___ Good for nothing	___ Opinions not valued	___ Unlovable
___ Can't trust anyone	___ Guilty	___ Out of control	___ Unloved
___ Cheap	___ Gutted	___ Overwhelmed	___ Unnecessary
___ Cheated	___ Hated	___ Out of touch	___ Unneeded
___ Condemned	___ Hate myself	___ Pathetic	___ Unnoticed
___ Confused	___ Helpless	___ Powerless	___ Unprotected
___ Conspired against	___ Hollow	___ Pressured	___ Unresponsive
___ Controlled	___ Hopeless	___ Pressured to perform	___ Unsafe
___ Cornered	___ Humiliated	___ Publicly shamed	___ Unseen
___ Cowardly	___ Hurt	___ Put down	___ Used
___ Crushed	___ Hysterical	___ Rage	___ Unsupported
___ Cut off	___ Ignored	___ Rejected	___ Unwanted
___ Deceived	___ Impure	___ Rejection Repulsed	___ Unworthy
___ Defeated	___ Inadequate	___ Resentful	___ Useless
___ Defenseless	___ Incompetent	___ Revenge	___ Violated
___ Defrauded	___ Indecent	___ Ridiculed	___ Vulnerable
___ Degraded	___ Inferior	___ Ruined	___ Walked on
___ Depressed	___ Infuriated	___ Sad	___ Wasted
___ Deprived	___ Inhibited	___ Scared	___ Weak
___ Desires were rejected	___ Insecure	___ Secluded	___ _____
___ Desperate	___ Insensitive to my needs	___ Self-disgust	___ _____
___ Despised	___ Insignificant	___ Shaken	___ _____
___ Despair	___ Isolated	___ Shamed	___ _____
___ Despondent	___ Invaded	___ Sick	___ _____
___ Destroyed	___ Invalidated	___ Stuck	___ _____
___ Devalued	___ Invisible	___ Stressed	___ _____
___ Didn't belong	___ Judged	___ Stupid	___ _____

© 2019, Joseph Saladino

www.ingramcontent.com/pod-product-compliance
Lightning Source LLC
Chambersburg PA
CBHW081157070526
44583CB00021B/2886